DEFENDING THE NATION

Defending the Nation

THE ARMY

John Hamilton
ABDO Publishing Company

visit us at
www.abdopublishing.com

Published by ABDO Publishing Company, 4940 Viking Drive, Edina, Minnesota 55435.
Copyright © 2007 by Abdo Consulting Group, Inc. International copyrights reserved in all
countries. No part of this book may be reproduced in any form without written permission from
the publisher. The Checkerboard Library™ is a trademark and logo of ABDO Publishing
Company.

Printed in the United States.

Cover Photos: front, U.S. Army; back, U.S. Air Force
Interior Photos: Corbis pp. 1, 8, 9, 12, 14, 15, 16, 17, 23; Getty Images p. 13; U.S. Air Force
     p. 19; U.S. Army pp. 5, 10-11, 20-21, 25, 27, 29

Series Coordinator: Megan M. Gunderson
Editors: Heidi M. Dahmes, Megan M. Gunderson
Art Direction & Cover Design: Neil Klinepier

Library of Congress Cataloging-in-Publication Data

Hamilton, John, 1959-
  The Army / John Hamilton.
     p. cm. -- (Defending the nation)
  Includes index.
  ISBN-13: 978-1-59679-754-3
  ISBN-10: 1-59679-754-1
  1. United States. Army--Juvenile literature. I. Title II. Series: Hamilton, John, 1959- .
Defending the nation.

  UA25.H26 2005
  355.00973--dc22

                                                                    2005028752

Contents

The U.S. Army

The U.S. military exists to protect America and its people. Today, it is among the most powerful militaries on Earth. The military is trained to kill and destroy enemies. But it also assists people in distress. After hurricanes, earthquakes, or other natural disasters strike, the U.S. military is often there to help.

The U.S. Army is one branch of the military. Its roots trace back to early American history. The U.S. Army defends against foreign invaders. It also serves in peacekeeping missions. And, it can send soldiers and equipment anywhere in the world if U.S. leaders think the country will benefit.

It is the army's job to preserve the peace and security of the United States. The men and women of today's U.S. Army are volunteers. They freely give their time, and sometimes their lives, to defend their country.

There are 175 streamers attached to the U.S. Army flag. Each one indicates the name and year of a campaign the army has participated in.

1775 - On June 14, the Continental Congress established the Continental army; on June 15, George Washington was named commander of the army.

1784 - On June 3, Congress officially created the U.S. Army.

1802 - The U.S. Military Academy at West Point was established.

1901 - Women were allowed to join the U.S. Army Nurse Corps.

1940 - Benjamin O. Davis Sr. became the first African-American general.

1944 - Dwight D. Eisenhower became a five-star general.

1973 - Conscription ended and the army became an all-volunteer force.

1988 - H. Norman Schwarzkopf became a four-star general.

1989 - Colin Powell became the first African-American chairman of the Joint Chiefs of Staff.

2005 - The National Guard assisted victims of Hurricane Katrina.

Fun Facts

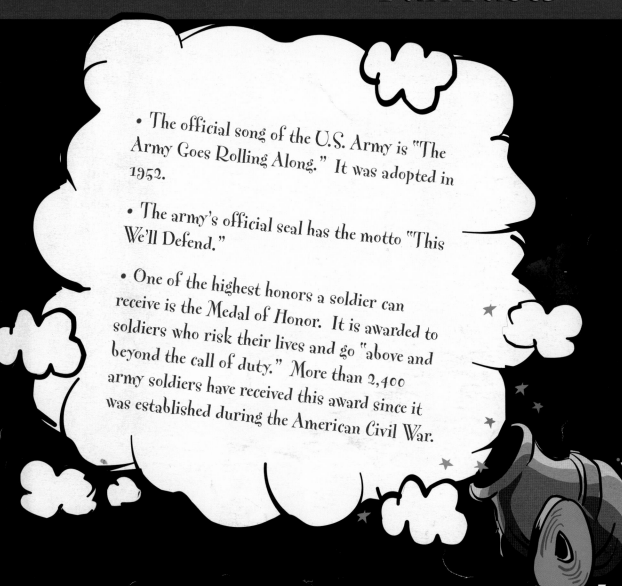

• The official song of the U.S. Army is "The Army Goes Rolling Along." It was adopted in 1952.

• The army's official seal has the motto "This We'll Defend."

• One of the highest honors a soldier can receive is the Medal of Honor. It is awarded to soldiers who risk their lives and go "above and beyond the call of duty." More than 2,400 army soldiers have received this award since it was established during the American Civil War.

History of the Army

Great Britain owned America's 13 original colonies. But the British government was too far away to fully protect its colonies. So, the settlers learned to protect themselves. To defend their homes and families, each colony formed groups of armed men called militias. Militiamen were not professional soldiers. Rather, they were ordinary citizens who used their own clothing and weapons when fighting.

In the 1760s, unfair British laws and taxes angered the colonists. This eventually led to Britain waging war against the colonies and America demanding independence. The first shots of the **Revolutionary War** were fired on April 19, 1775. The Battles of Lexington and Concord were fought between the British army and the Massachusetts militiamen.

Some of the militiamen who fought at the Battles of Lexington and Concord were also called minutemen. They were trained to be ready "at a minute's notice."

The militias fought bravely. However, American leaders realized the need for a unified army that would be more reliable and better trained. So on June 14, 1775, the **Continental Congress** established the Continental army.

The Continental army was a national force created to protect all 13 colonies. The militias were still important. But now they worked together with a more permanent armed force. A combination of militiamen and Continental army soldiers fought in the **Revolutionary War**. More than 250,000 men served in these forces, many in both.

Music has been an important part of the U.S. Army since the Revolutionary War. Today, there are 34 army bands.

The United States won its independence from Great Britain in 1783. The same year, the Continental army was **disbanded**. But the government quickly realized that a permanent army was necessary, even in peacetime. So, the U.S. Army was established on June 3, 1784. This peacetime military was needed to "provide for the common defense" and to protect America's borders.

Throughout its long history, the U.S. Army has fought many wars. During the American **Civil War**, the Union army reached a strength of 1 million men. Another 4 million soldiers helped win **World War I**. The army has also played a large part in the current struggle against **terrorism**. Today, army soldiers are stationed in countries throughout the world, including Iraq and Afghanistan.

The number of people in the army changes constantly. In times of peace, there are fewer soldiers. After the **Revolutionary War** ended, only a few hundred soldiers were needed. But during **World War II**, more than 8 million Americans served in the army. Currently, there are about 700,000 active-duty and reserve soldiers in the U.S. Army.

Countries sometimes use a draft, or conscription, in times of war. In the United States, the draft is a system of selecting and requiring male citizens to serve in the armed forces. The United States drafted soldiers to fight in the American **Civil War** and **World War II**, among others. Most recently, conscription ended in 1973. This means that the U.S. Army is currently an all-volunteer force.

The U.S. Army Corps of Engineers

The U.S. Army Corps of Engineers is responsible for both civil and military engineering projects. It was established on June 16, 1775. Since then, the corps has participated in major construction projects worldwide. Today, it employs engineers, biologists, geologists, and other experts.

The corps is in charge of designing and constructing military buildings. In the early 1940s, it built the Pentagon. The corps has also been responsible for improving harbors, building lighthouses, and constructing bridges.

Flood protection is another main job of the corps. It was heavily involved in helping restore the Gulf Coast region after Hurricane Katrina struck in 2005. For all projects, the corps attempts to protect and sustain the surrounding environment.

Great Army Commanders

Many great soldiers have bravely led the U.S. Army in times of need. General George Washington became commander of the Continental army on June 15, 1775. Washington was courageous, devoted, and patient. He led the army to victory against the British during the **Revolutionary War**. In 1789, Washington was elected the first president of the United States.

George Washington was president of the United States from 1789 to 1797.

President Dwight D. Eisenhower was another skilled army leader. He graduated from the U.S. Military Academy at West Point in 1915. During **World War II**, he helped lead America and its **allies** to victory. And in 1944, he was made a five-star general. Eight years later, the popular general was elected president.

General H. Norman Schwarzkopf graduated from West Point in 1956. He then fought in the **Vietnam War**. In 1988, he became a four-star general. Three years later, he led Operation Desert Storm during the **Persian Gulf War**. During this conflict, he commanded the military forces of both the United States and its **allies**.

Schwarzkopf earned the nickname "Stormin' Norman" for his bold actions during the Persian Gulf War.

Women Soldiers

When the Continental army was formed, its members were almost entirely men. It was rare to see women in the armed forces. Beginning in 1901, women could join the U.S. Army Nurse Corps. Near the end of **World War I**, more than 20,000 women were serving as nurses.

In 1997, Claudia J. Kennedy became the first woman to earn the rank of lieutenant general in the U.S. Army.

During **World War II**, the formation of the Women's Army Corps (WAC) allowed more than 150,000 women to serve as official members of the army. At first, women still had mainly nursing and administrative roles. But as time went by, they began taking jobs as electricians, mechanics, and air traffic controllers. The WAC program ended in 1978. At that time, the male and female forces were combined.

Today, thousands of women proudly serve as soldiers in the U.S. Army. They have nearly the same opportunities and pay as men. Their duties sometimes put them into combat zones. Almost one of every seven soldiers in the armed forces is a woman.

Since 1993, male and female army recruits have participated in basic training together.

Equality in the Army

African Americans have served in every war America has fought. Many served during the **Revolutionary War** and the **War of 1812**. But after 1820, they were forbidden to **enlist**. Then during the American **Civil War**, African Americans were again permitted to serve. In that war, more than 180,000 Union army soldiers were African American.

Despite this loyal service, African-American soldiers were not treated equally. They usually lived, ate, and fought apart from white troops. And, they were often commanded by white officers. There were no African-American generals until Benjamin O. Davis Sr. achieved the rank in 1940. Then in 1948, President Harry S. Truman ordered that all soldiers be given equal treatment and opportunities.

Benjamin O. Davis Sr. became a brigadier general in 1940. His son became the first African-American lieutenant general in 1965.

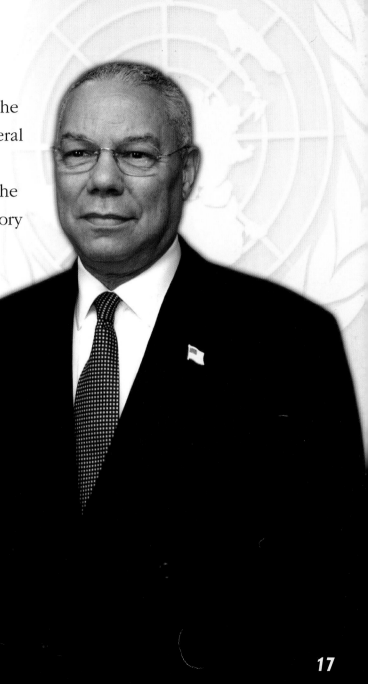

Today, there are many opportunities for minorities in the army. From 1989 to 1993, General Colin Powell served as the first African-American chairman of the Joint Chiefs of Staff. This advisory group consists of one representative from each of the major branches of the military. The leaders serve as a connection between the armed forces and the government.

Colin Powell also served as the first African-American secretary of state from 2001 to 2005.

Organization

The U.S. Army is organized by hierarchy. That means there are many levels of authority. In a school, there are student teachers, regular teachers, assistant principals, and principals. In the army, there are ranks of **enlisted** soldiers and officers. Generals are officers who make very big decisions, like school principals.

The head of the military is the president of the United States. He or she is called the commander in chief. The **Founding Fathers** wanted to be sure that the military did not have too much control. So, they put the power in the hands of elected officials. That is one reason the head of the army is the president. The president is a **civilian**, not a member of the military.

Eighty-five percent of soldiers enter the army as enlistees. These soldiers start as privates. Commissioned officers make up the other 15 percent of new soldiers. They usually enter the army as second lieutenants, most often after receiving a college degree.

Ranks

There are many ranks for soldiers in the U.S. Army. A rank is a level of responsibility. Soldiers can move up in rank by showing leadership skills. Promotions also depend on service length, education, and battle experience.

Officer Ranks

Second Lieutenant (O-1)

First Lieutenant (O-2)

Captain (O-3)

Major (O-4)

Lieutenant Colonel (O-5)

Colonel (O-6)

Brigadier General (O-7)

Major General (O-8)

Lieutenant General (O-9)

General (O-10)

General of the Army
(Wartime only)

Warrant Officer Ranks

Warrant Officer 1 (W-1)

Chief Warrant Officer 2 (W-2)

Chief Warrant Officer 3 (W-3)

Chief Warrant Officer 4 (W-4)

Chief Warrant Officer (W-5)

Enlisted Ranks

Private (E-1)

Private (E-2)

Private First Class (E-3)

Corporal (E-4)

Specialist (E-4)

Sergeant (E-5)

Staff Sergeant (E-6)

Sergeant First Class (E-7)

Master Sergeant (E-8)

First Sergeant (E-8)

Sergeant Major (E-9)

Command Sergeant Major (E-9)

Sergeant Major of the Army (E-9)

The letter and number next to each rank indicates a person's pay grade.

Training

Only U.S. citizens or legal **immigrants** may join the U.S. Army. Both men and women are welcome to **enlist**, but they must be between 17 and 34 years old. The army prefers enlistees who have already graduated from high school.

New soldiers, or recruits, must go through a program called Basic Combat Training. In nine weeks, recruits become more physically fit and learn how to take orders.

In basic training, recruits learn the Seven Core Army Values. These values are loyalty, duty, respect, selfless service, honor, integrity, and personal courage.

They also learn how to use weapons such as rifles and grenades. When their training is complete, recruits graduate in a special ceremony. Then, they are officially soldiers in the U.S. Army!

After graduation, soldiers move on to Advanced Individual Training (AIT). In this program, soldiers learn the skills they will need to successfully perform their specific army duties. There are 17 AIT schools, including Infantry School, Engineer School, and Military Police School.

For those who choose to advance their career, the army offers further training. Training in various fields occurs at specialized schools. These include Airborne School, Drill Sergeant School, and Defense Language Institute. Leadership training is also available for those soldiers interested in advancing in rank.

Army officers require even more education than **enlisted** soldiers. Some future officers attend Officer Candidate School. Others study at public or private military institutions across the nation.

The U.S. Military Academy at West Point, New York, was established in 1802. West Point admits students for both academic and physical strength. But the school focuses on teaching leadership skills. More than 50,000 officers have graduated from the program. Throughout history, many of the army's highest-ranking officers have been West Point graduates.

Since 1916, the Army Reserve Officers' Training Corps (ROTC) has been another training ground for army officers. The ROTC program takes place in high schools and colleges across America. Students take courses in leadership and the military. These lessons allow them to become army officers. The majority of officers in the active-duty and reserve armed forces come from the ROTC program.

West Point is located along the Hudson River. This provides a location for athletic training, such as rowing.

The Army National Guard

The Army National Guard is a part of the U.S. Army. It is equipped just like the regular army. The National Guard also uses the same ranking system. Today, there are about 350,000 soldiers in the National Guard.

Unlike the regular army, individual states command the National Guard. This means a state governor can order National Guard troops to help during emergencies, such as natural disasters. In September 2005, the National Guard assisted Hurricane Katrina victims. Troops also helped restore law and order in the Gulf Coast region.

In addition to assisting disaster relief efforts, National Guard soldiers have many other duties. They are sometimes used to control public disorder or fight forest fires.

Although the National Guard is commanded by the states, the president can order it to help the regular army at any time. Since the **terrorist** attacks on September 11, 2001, thousands of National Guard troops have helped provide national security. Many have also been employed in combat during the invasion and occupation of Iraq. And, they are used around the world as peacekeeping troops.

The Army Reserve is another part of the U.S. Army. After **enlistment**, reserve soldiers train for six months. Then, they return to their **civilian** jobs. One weekend each month, reserve soldiers have Unit Training at a local Army Reserve Center. And for two weeks each year, they participate in Field Training Exercises. Army Reserve units are always ready to be sent wherever assistance is needed.

After Hurricane Katrina, National Guard soldiers dropped bags of rocks and sand from helicopters to prevent further flooding in New Orleans, Louisiana.

On the Battlefield

One of the army's most valuable weapons is its infantry. Infantry personnel are the soldiers who fight on the ground. Army soldiers are very well trained. They are prepared to follow orders and to think creatively on the battlefield.

Army soldiers have many weapons they can use to fight wars. Infantry troops rely on rifles, pistols, rocket launchers, mines, and other deadly weapons. And, they depend on radio and **satellite** communications systems to fight more effectively.

The army also uses large weapons systems, such as tanks. These armored vehicles can be used to destroy enemy forces. Tanks such as the Bradley M2A3 Infantry Fighting Vehicle help protect troops on the ground.

Ground troops understand the danger posed by enemy artillery. Well-aimed artillery can destroy targets many miles away. So, the U.S. Army prepares itself with artillery such as the M119A2 Howitzer. This weapon shoots explosives deep into enemy territory.

The army relies on helicopters as both rescue vehicles and weapons. Helicopters also transport soldiers to and from the battlefield. The AH-64D Apache Longbow helicopter has high-tech missiles, rockets, and guns. It also uses advanced navigation equipment.

AH-64D Apache Longbow

Bradley Infantry Fighting Vehicle

Into the Future

The U.S. Army is more than 200 years old. It has fought in hundreds of conflicts. And, it remains among the most powerful armies in the world. The army's mission is to protect and support America and its citizens.

Today, the global war on **terrorism** is a serious threat to America. The U.S. Army is fighting this challenge by becoming faster and lighter. It is now better able to quickly send troops anywhere in the world. This helps not only in wartime, but also in response to natural disasters.

To quickly overcome new dangers, the army relies heavily on the latest technology. This includes advanced weapons and communications systems. However, nothing can replace well-trained soldiers.

The army is committed to training brave soldiers who will defend the United States. Soldiers will be armed with the most advanced weapons and equipment. With the best soldiers leading the way, the U.S. Army will be able to meet whatever challenges the future holds.

New technology allows soldiers to use satellites to send and receive photos and videos anywhere in the world.

allies - people or countries that agree to help each other in times of need.

civil war - a war between groups in the same country. The United States of America and the Confederate States of America fought a civil war from 1861 to 1865.

civilian - of or relating to something nonmilitary.

Continental Congress - the body of representatives that spoke for and acted on behalf of the 13 colonies.

disband - to break up something that is organized.

enlist - to join the armed forces voluntarily. An enlistee is a person who enlists for military service.

Founding Fathers - the men who attended the Constitutional Convention in Philadelphia, Pennsylvania, in 1787. They helped write the U.S. Constitution.

immigration - entry into another country to live. A person who immigrates is called an immigrant.

Persian Gulf War - from January 16, 1991, to February 28, 1991. A war in the Persian Gulf to liberate Kuwait from Iraqi forces.

Revolutionary War - from 1775 to 1783. A war for independence between Great Britain and its North American colonies. The colonists won and created the United States of America.

satellite - a manufactured object that orbits Earth.

terrorism - the use of terror, violence, or threats to frighten people into action. A person who commits an act of terrorism is called a terrorist.

Vietnam War - from 1957 to 1975. A long, failed attempt by the United States to stop North Vietnam from taking over South Vietnam.

War of 1812 - from 1812 to 1814. A war fought between the United States and Great Britain over shipping rights and the capture of U.S. soldiers.

World War I - from 1914 to 1918, fought in Europe. Great Britain, France, Russia, the United States, and their allies were on one side. Germany, Austria-Hungary, and their allies were on the other side.

World War II - from 1939 to 1945, fought in Europe, Asia, and Africa. Great Britain, France, the United States, the Soviet Union, and their allies were on one side. Germany, Italy, Japan, and their allies were on the other side.

Web Sites

To learn more about the U.S. Army, visit ABDO Publishing Company on the World Wide Web at **www.abdopublishing.com**. Web sites about the U.S. Army are featured on our Book Links page. These links are routinely monitored and updated to provide the most current information available.

Index

A
American Civil War 10, 11, 16
Army National Guard 24
Army Reserve 10, 22, 25
Army Reserve Officers' Training Corps 22

C
conscription 11
Continental Congress 9

D
Davis, General Benjamin O., Sr. 16
disaster relief 4, 24, 28

E
Eisenhower, President Dwight D. 12
enemies 4, 10, 24, 26, 28

H
helicopters 27

M
militias 8, 9

P
Persian Gulf War 13
Powell, General Colin 17

R
Revolutionary War 8, 9, 10, 12, 16

S
satellites 26
Schwarzkopf, General H. Norman 13
September 11, 2001 24

T
tanks 26
Truman, President Harry S. 16

U
U.S. Army Nurse Corps 14
U.S. Military Academy 12, 13, 22

V
Vietnam War 13

W
War of 1812 16
Washington, President George 12
weapons 8, 21, 26, 27, 28
Women's Army Corps 14
World War I 10, 14
World War II 10, 11, 12, 14